NeXTmodernism

Alejandro Saint-Barthélemy

[¥€$]

*The culture of liquid modernity
has no "populace" to enlighten and ennoble;
it does, however, have clients to seduce.*
(Zygmunt Bauman)

[● ~ *]

*Content is a glimpse of something,
an encounter like a flash.*
(Willem de Kooning)

[???]

Most postmodern, contemporary art
is a vomit of silliness.
Paradoxically enough,
Marcel Duchamp
originated it as the supremacy of intellect
over craft and emotion.

NeXTmodernism cuts through the soul
of both tendencies
and it's as silly
(one sentence per book,
in the case of NeXTmodernist literature)
as intellectual
(self-aware, lucid, clairvoyant, insightful...
due to the terminal state of culture
under consumerism).

[0]

*Art has the lovely habit of
ruining all artistic theories.*
(Marcel Duchamp)

[00]

MOSCA

Modern
Original
Shocking

=

Contemporary
Art.

[[[000]]]

MODN

Modern
Original
Decorative

=

NeXTmodernism.

[007]

We know that the nature of genius is to provide idiots with ideas twenty years later.
(Louis Aragon)

[1]

A NeXTmodernist author
(entrepreneur ;)
is satisfied as long as the reader
(consumer ;)
purchases their book.

In Money we trust.

[2]

After centuries of canvases, sculptures, poems,
cathedrals, novels, plays, sonatas…
we have become terribly lucid.

After a century of anti-art,
we have become too terribly lucid.

We see that the best art of the 21st century
can be found in movies, manga, cartoons, anime,
TV series, tattoos, popular music, photography,
grafitti,
fashion (8th art), video games (9th art)…
and not whatever worn out, dead art medium
the foolish pedantics still hold to.

[3]

First artistic movement openly oriented to the consumer.

It is good to remember that the best artistic movement of the 21st, so far, has been the art market itself.

*Between the good and the new,
I always choose the new.*
(César Aira).

There were enough great artists in the past.
Too many masterpieces have been done already.
Welcome to the 21st century.

Gucci Gang.

INSTRUCTIONS:

(1) Pick up a book from the NeXTmodernist shelf at the bookstore.

(2) Decide if you like the artwork and/or title enough
(if not, pick up another one and retry).

(3) The content says the same as the title, so there's no need to open it.

(4)
Purchase it.

[5]

A NeXTmodernist,
even if they have created any themself,
doesn't believe in masterpieces
being able to be created
in a world where faith has been vanished:
God,
humankind,
artistic inmortality,
civilisation…
makes us shrug, grin or cry
(everything but nod).

[6]

We should remember that all the arts
are fine arts
and all the arts
decorative arts.
(Oscar Wilde)

Proto-NeXTmodernism == Ambient music.

NeXTmodernism == Candy floss.

[007]

Nowadays,
Arthur Rimbaud
would be in an electronic band.

Nowadays,
William Shakespeare
would be a screenwriter.

Nowadays,
Leonardo da Vinci
would be a tattoo artist,
app developer,
graphic designer...

Nowdays,
Lautréamont
would be a poet.

Nowadays,
Miguel de Cervantes
would be a novelist.

[7]

*In the old days,
books had awful covers and marvelous content;
nowadays, the opposite happens.*
(Leopardi)

That was said in the first half of the 19th century.
Picture il signore Giacomo in Barnes & Noble today...
passing out on his way out of the store...

[8]

*The true vanguardist is unnaceptable,
infamous
and illegible.*
(César Aira)

[9]

*Being a vanguardist has always meant,
and will always mean,
to not accept that the good is good
and the bad is bad,
and invent a new definition
of what's good and bad.*
(César Aira)

[10]

The point of NeXTmodernism
is to always be a step ahead,
like Duchamp's contemporary art
has proven to be.

It doesn't get any more modern
and in tune with contemporary society
(globalised and digitized)
than an empty book,
for, paraphrasing (and actualizing)
Guy Debord…:
*The decline of being into having,
and having into merely appearing.*

We're fated to pretend... ♪♫♬

[11]

The Oxford English Dictionary's definition
of the word *piñata* is illuminating
and in accordance with the intentions of
NeXTmodernism:
*A decorated figure of an animal
containing toys and sweets
that is suspended from a height and broken open
by blindfolded children
as part of a celebration.*

[12]

The majority of writers demand to be read;
the minority, to be memorised.

NeXTmodernists demand to be collected.

[13]

*People often talk as if there was an opposition
between what is beautiful and what is useful.
There is no opposition to beauty except ugliness:
all things are either beautiful or ugly,
and utility will be always on the side
of the beautiful thing.*
(Oscar Wilde)

[14]

The average attention span for the notoriously
ill-focused goldfish is 9 seconds,
but according to a study from
Microsoft Corp.,
people now generally lose concentration after 8
seconds,
highlighting the affects of an increasingly
digitized lifestyle on the brain.

NeXTmodernism demands less than 5 seconds.

¥€$, we can.

[15]

NeXTmodernism is
the democratization of fine arts:
the end of psychological misery,
style,
talent,
genius...

[16]

NeXTmodernist books cost ¥€$7.77.
In contemporary art, as in life,
it is better to be lucky than good.

NeXTmodernist books cannot be digitized.

An e-book cannot be in a shelf
and/or
used as decoration.

Proto-NeXTmodernist books can be read.
This manifesto should be read,
to understand the movement theoretically
(though it is always better to do so instinctively,
as it goes with everything).
Beyond this,
NeXTmodernist authors
only recommend the reading of their books
under the influence of absinthe, ayahuasca…

[17]

How to choose a NeXTmodernist author
over another
to collect their complete works
or just a NeXTmodernist book
over another one?
AAAA:

    1) **A**rtwork.
    2) **A**uthor's genre.
    3) **A**uthor's nom de plume.
    4) **A**mount of pages.

[18]

Notorius examples of NeXTmodernism:

1) *The End of Faith*, by Sam Harris.
If only it was written in the Medieval Period, it wouldn't be on this list, but writing such an essay in a world where our gods are celebrities and afterlife a TV series, well, seems quite decorative to me...

2) *Bad Feminist*, by Roxanne Gay.
The title and the cover are better than the book. It would decorate nicely on an Ikea shelf on display. Great marketing move (a black, bisexual woman calling herself a bad feminist in such delicate and political correct times as ours...)

3) *The Opposite of Loneliness*, by Marina Keegan. Great marketing, branding move: a young, overachiever, rich, slim, trendy, hip, hipster, cute, friendly, nice, Yale kiddo with a job at the New Yorker waiting for her, dying in a car accident, with her very boyfriend driving and making it through... sells really, really well... but opening the book leads to disappointment, for it doesn't get any better than the cover, title and story I just told you.

4) Most best-sellers.

5) Most indie books.

6) Damien Hirts's spot paintings.

7) Most post-modern art.

8) Maurizio Cattelan's Caribbean Biennal.

9) Mr. Brainwash.

10) And so on and so forth...

[19]

Books are toys for adults.
 (César Aira)

[20]

*In the old days,
books were written by men of letters
and read by the public.
Nowadays,
books are written by the public
and read by nobody.*
(Oscar Wilde)

[21]

Writers ought to be regarded as wrongdoers
who deserve to be acquitted
or pardoned
only in the rarest cases:
that would be a way to keep books from getting
out of hand.
(Friedrich Nietzsche)

[22]

NeXTmodernism is the law.
NeXTmodernism under money.

[23]
NeXT

[24]
NeXT

[25]

NeXT

[26]

NeXTmodernism.

NeXTmodernist Manifesto.

[28]

*Those are my principles,
and if you don't like them...
well, I have others.
(Groucho Marx)*

(^_^) o 自自 o (^_^)

<(((">

><>

<*)))-{

><(((*>

@}-;-'---

@>-->--

www.ingramcontent.com/pod-product-compliance
Lightning Source LLC
Chambersburg PA
CBHW030102230526
45471CB00003B/1210